VIEWPOINTS AND PERSPECTIVES

VIEWPOINTS ON THE BATTLE OF BUNKER HILL

PART OF THE PERSPECTIVES LIBRARY

KRISTIN J. RUSSO

Published in the United States of America by Cherry Lake Publishing
Ann Arbor, Michigan
www.cherrylakepublishing.com

Reading Adviser: Marla Conn MS, Ed., Literacy specialist, Read-Ability, Inc.

Photo Credits: ©Design Pics/Newscom, cover (left); ©moonisblack/Getty Images, cover (middle); ©Everett Historical/Newscom, cover (right); ©Design Pics/Newscom, 1 (left); ©moonisblack/Getty Images, 1 (middle); ©Everett Historical/Newscom, 1 (right); ©Design Pics/Newscom, 4; ©Picture History/Newscom, 7; ©Picture History/Newscom, 9; ©duncan1890/Getty Images, 11; ©Design Pics/Newscom, 13; ©Liszt Collection/Newscom, 15; ©moonisblack/Getty Images, 18; ©Prisma/Newscom, 19; ©The Print Collector Heritage Images/Newscom, 21; ©Everett Historical/Shutterstock, 23; ©akg-images/Newscom/Newscom, 24; ©NewscomThe Print Collector Heritage Images/Newscom, 27; ©World History Archive/Newscom, 29; ©Everett Historical/Newscom, 32; ©bauhaus1000/Getty Images, 33; ©GeorgiosArt/Getty Images, 36; ©Tichnor Bros. Inc./Wikimedia, 38; ©Picture History/Newscom, 41; ©Prisma/Newscom, 43; ©Picture History/Newscom, 44; ©Prisma/Newscom, 45; ©World History Archive/Newscom, 45; ©Liszt Collection/Newscom, 46

Library of Congress Cataloging-in-Publication Data has been filed and is available at catalog.loc.gov

Cherry Lake Publishing would like to acknowledge the work of The Partnership for 21st Century Learning.
Please visit *www.p21.org* for more information.

Printed in the United States of America
Corporate Graphics

TABLE OF CONTENTS

In this book, you will read about the Battle of Bunker Hill from three perspectives. Each perspective is based on real things that happened to real people who lived in or near Boston in 1775. As you'll see, the same event can look different depending on one's point of view.

THOMAS GAGE

BRITISH GENERAL

Did the colonists really think that their little Tea Party would go unanswered? How weak do they think His Majesty's government is? Naturally their **treasonous** vandalism would cause a backlash. Little did they know how **intolerable** that backlash would be.

I am commander-in-chief of all British forces in North America and have been military governor of Massachusetts since last year, 1774.

All who know me know that I try to negotiate **diplomatically** first. They also know that I am not afraid to use the strong arm of **artillery** when necessary. I take my job as adviser to **Parliament** seriously. My reports of the colonists' activities may be critical—some might even say unsympathetic—but they are objective. I have lived on the North American continent for a long time. I served with the British military here as long ago as the **Seven Years' War** in the 1760s. I know what these lawless people need. They need a strong, swift response to any and all mischief and wrongdoing.

THINK ABOUT IT

Determine the point of this paragraph and pick out one piece of evidence that supports it.

In 1773, Samuel Adams's secret group, the **Sons of Liberty**, dumped more than 340 chests of tea into Boston Harbor to avoid paying the required tax on tea. Parliament acted swiftly, and by 1774 it had imposed stricter laws. Finally, they are taking a stand against the colonists' lawless ways. This will make my job easier.

The Tea Party proved to legislators in England what they had long suspected—that the instigators of the colonial rebellion are right here in Boston. Thus, the people of Boston have been punished harshly. As they should be.

Some call Parliament's new laws the Intolerable Acts. Others call them the Coercive Acts. Whatever name they are given, the outcome is the same. They have caused the colonists great suffering. Parliament has revoked the Massachusetts Colony's charter—a charter that has been in place since 1691—and instead has created a military government of which I am in charge. Naturally, town meetings are illegal without my approval.

In addition, Boston Harbor is closed until the colonists pay for the lost tea. This makes it impossible

BRITISH SHIPS ANCHORED IN BOSTON HARBOR FIRED ON COLONISTS AS THEY FORTIFIED BREED'S HILL.

for local merchants to import and export goods. How they will make the payment with this sanction in place is their problem. I have troubles enough of my own.

The **Quartering** Act seems to anger the colonists the most. If there is to be military rule in Boston, there must be a place for British soldiers to stay. The colonists who are disloyal to the Crown resist this by

WHAT WAS THE QUARTERING ACT?

When the Quartering Act was passed by Parliament on May 15, 1765, it required colonists to provide British soldiers living in their homes with such items as bedding, beer, candles, cider, firewood, and eating utensils. All 13 colonies protested this legislation, and only Pennsylvania agreed to follow the law.

MANY MINUTEMEN WHO FOUGHT TO PROTECT THEIR OWN TOWNS JOINED FORCES AND FORMED A MILITIA TO PROTECT BOSTON AND SURROUNDING TOWNS. MILITIAMEN WHO WERE ONCE MINUTEMEN PLAYED AN IMPORTANT ROLE AT THE BATTLE OF BUNKER HILL.

refusing to repair vacant buildings where my soldiers could live in relative comfort. Instead, my troops are camped outdoors like livestock on Boston Common. This is intolerable! Therefore, I have seen to it that the Quartering Act is expanded. It now requires private citizens to house British soldiers in their homes. Colonial wives are required to feed and serve my soldiers. They must even repair their uniforms and do their laundry. Naturally, they consider this an outrage. We'll see now how quickly they will provide suitable **barracks** for these men!

I feel these Boston colonists completely overreact to the right and just rule of the Crown. For example, after I ordered my soldiers to march on Lexington and Concord in April 1775 in search of stores of artillery that the colonists had hidden away, how did they respond? By chasing my soldiers with bayonets at daybreak on the Lexington town green. Hours later, they fired their muskets upon them in the town of

Concord! Following these skirmishes, the Crown saw fit to increase my troops in Boston to 5,000. The colonists will surely not be so foolish as to oppose an army of this size.

THE BATTLE OF CONCORD WAS FOUGHT ON THE GROUNDS OF THE OLD MANSE, THE FAMILY HOMESTEAD OF RALPH WALDO EMERSON. TO THE EMERSONS, THE EVENT WAS KNOWN AS "THE BATTLE IN THE BACKYARD."

Now my goal as commander is to occupy Dorchester Heights. From this strategic spot, it is possible to view the city and surrounding towns. Breed's Hill and Bunker Hill are also important strategic spots. We will occupy those areas next. With the British military stationed atop these hills, the low-lying towns and villages will fall under our supervision and, if need be, gunfire.

If the colonists have plans to organize a militia and repeat the reckless behavior they showed in April at Lexington and Concord, we will surely know about it. We will be able to defuse the situation quickly. I have dispatched 2,300 troops under the command of Major General William Howe to complete the takeover of Dorchester Heights. I expect this to happen quickly and without resistance.

What's this? I have received word that a gathering of colonial militia has been forming at Breed's Hill since darkness fell on June 16. They are building

On March 4, 1776, under orders from General George Washington, General John Thomas took control of Dorchester Heights with 2,000 troops and cannons stolen from Fort Ticonderoga.

defensive fortifications. And by "defensive fortifications," I mean they have set up railings they have stuffed with hedges and hay. Surely, they do not think this will discourage the Royal army. However, this provocation will have to be dealt with immediately. It will put off our plans for overtaking Dorchester Heights. I have sent Major General Howe and his troops to deal with this problem.

As they neared Breed's Hill, they saw the colonists had mustered a small group of only about 1,200 militiamen. Did they really think they could overcome our 2,300 troops? Not to mention the cannonade that fire upon them from warships anchored in the Charles River. Where do these people get their gall?

They have dug trenches and refuse to leave Breed's Hill and Bunker Hill. Although British troops far outnumbered them, Howe reported that the colonial militia had the advantage of height from atop the hills. The colonists began volleying artillery at

MOST OF THE FIGHTING AT THE BATTLE OF BUNKER HILL TOOK PLACE ON NEARBY BREED'S HILL IN CHARLESTOWN. THE BRITISH WANTED BOTH HILLS SO THAT THEY COULD SET UP CANNONS AND AIM THEM AT THE CITY OF BOSTON.

SECOND SOURCE

Find another source describing the beginnings of the Battle of Bunker Hill and compare the information there to the information in this source.

Howe's advancing troops at about 3 o'clock in the afternoon on June 17. It is now June 18 and I can still hear skirmishes!

According to Howe, British soldiers climbed the hills side by side only to succumb time after time to the colonial militia's artillery fire. Howe reported that the battle turned in his favor once he switched from row advancements to columns. By this time, the colonial militia had run out of artillery. They were forced to retreat. Both Breed's Hill and Bunker Hill were taken by British troops. How could they ever doubt our dominance? Yes, we took heavy casualties compared to the colonists' militia. More than 1,000 British soldiers were killed or wounded, including 92 officers, compared to only about 140 colonial militiamen killed. Unfortunately, the colonists have taken encouragement from this skirmish, though they clearly lost.

This has resulted in a loss of morale among my own men. Howe writes that the taking of Breed's Hill and Bunker Hill "was too dearly bought." Howe lost so many men in this fight that he will need to refortify his troops before he can advance on Dorchester Heights. The colonial militia of Boston will surely learn in the end which army has the most power. The British Royal military is the most powerful in the world.

2

SALEM POOR

FORMER SLAVE AND COLONIAL MILITIAMAN

I shove a handful of hay between two railings and pack it down tightly. We've been here all night, digging trenches and fortifying them with fencing. I have met a new friend. His name is David Daily. He hails from Lisbon, New Hampshire. He is one of Colonel John Stark's men. David points out a spot that needs more fill. Together, we close the gap. Though our fortifications

THE COLONISTS REACHED THE TOP OF BOTH BREED'S HILL AND BUNKER HILL WELL BEFORE THE BRITISH. THE COLONISTS WERE FORCED TO RETREAT WHEN THEY RAN OUT OF AMMUNITION.

are made from primitive materials, they are strong and well made. We are dug in tight. If the redcoats want Breed's Hill, they are going to have to fight for it.

The sun rises on June 17, 1775. We should be exhausted from our overnight work. But instead we are jittery with anticipation. Colonel William Prescott received word that the British had planned to take Dorchester Heights today. Our plan is to distract the redcoats by occupying Breed's Hill and Bunker Hill. This will pull their attention away from Dorchester and give the colonial militia more time to seize it.

It fills us with courage to know that we are not alone in this fight. I have heard that since the Battles of Lexington and Concord, other colonies in Massachusetts, New Hampshire, Rhode Island, and Connecticut have been sending men to Boston to help. David Daily is one of those men.

ANALYZE THIS

Analyze two of the accounts of the Battles of Lexington and Concord. How are they alike? How are they different?

THE TYPE OF FORTIFICATION THE COLONISTS BUILT ON BREED'S HILL WAS CALLED A REDOUBT. IT WAS MORE THAN 6 FEET (2 METERS) HIGH.

I have heard that there are up to 15,000 colonial militiamen in or near the city. But I don't see them here. Right now Breed's Hill holds only about 1,200 men. From my point of view, it is hard to guess the number of militiamen that hold Bunker Hill. When the redcoats arrive, it looks as though they have double our lot, about 2,300. While it is alarming to face an army that is double our size, this means the plan is working. If the redcoats are here to engage in skirmish with us, then they are not at Dorchester Heights. With these numbers, it won't exactly be a fair fight. But then, those redcoats have to fight uphill. We have the advantage. I think. I hope.

It's not like I have never had to fight an uphill battle before. I'm a former slave, you know. I used to work on a farm in Andover. It was run by Rebecca and John Poor. I bought my freedom when I was a young man, only 22. Cost me a mighty sum—27 pounds. It would take a free man about a year to earn this sum. It

BRITISH FORCES CLIMBING BREED'S HILL AND BUNKER HILL CARRIED 60 POUNDS (27 KILOGRAMS) OF EQUIPMENT AS THEY MADE THEIR WAY THROUGH TALL GRASS AND OVER UNEVEN GROUND.

AFTER LOSSES AT LEXINGTON AND CONCORD, BRITISH FORCES WERE INTENT ON TAKING BUNKER HILL, BREED'S HILL, AND DORCHESTER HEIGHTS SO THAT BOSTON COULD BE BETTER CONTROLLED.

certainly took me a very long time to save the price of my freedom. Now that I have my freedom, I'll fight to keep it. I will no longer accept tyranny in any form, for me, my wife, or my newborn son.

I mustered with the men at the Battle of Concord. Soon after, I enlisted and was assigned to Captain James Frye's Massachusetts Minutemen regiment. Our regiment is 850 men strong. On Colonel Prescott's orders, we marched from Cambridge to Charlestown last night.

Colonel Prescott is concerned that we are low on artillery. While each man has at least a musket, it is true that we are low on ammunition and gunpowder. Prescott wishes us to hold fire until the redcoats are close. He is hoping to conserve the weaponry that we have. Our orders are to hold fire until the redcoats are in range. Someone told me that Prescott has ordered us to hold fire, "Until you see the whites of their eyes."

The redcoats are on the move. They are marching

up the hill now. Why would they do this? They are defenseless against our artillery. The fighting is wild! Cannons roar like thunder. Acrid smoke fills the air. When the smoke clears, it is obvious the redcoats have taken many more casualties than we militiamen have. This makes us bold!

The redcoats charge again! Our stores of artillery are still adequate. The enemy is met with a great volley of bullets. We, too, are met with a brutal attack. We are starting to feel the impact of being outnumbered. But we will not give up. The fighting goes on for hours. Many of our men fall. But not as many as theirs. We will not be vanquished!

SECOND SOURCE

Find another source describing the British advance toward Bunker Hill and compare the information there to the information in this source.

The redcoats surge a third time. They have changed their strategy. Before, they marched toward us in rows. They were easily picked off by gunfire. This

OF THE 2,300 BRITISH TROOPS FIGHTING AT BUNKER HILL, 268 SOLDIERS AND OFFICERS WERE KILLED AND 828 WERE WOUNDED.

time they approach in columns. They are no longer easy targets. Our ammunition is nearly gone. We have used all of our gunpowder. But I am not ready to give up. When the redcoats reach the top of the hill, we fight in hand-to-hand combat. They find we are determined, and we fight with all our might. "This day will be ours!" I cry. British soldiers and officers land dead at my feet. I will not give up!

David Daily and I are out of ammunition. We dig up rocks and throw them like bullets. We also use our bayonets. We would all fight to the death. But Prescott sees that the cause is a hopeless one without gunpowder and bullets. Prescott calls for a retreat. We obey orders and retreat to the bottom of the hill. The British may have taken Breed's Hill and Bunker Hill on this day, but we have proven ourselves to be worthy opponents for the so-called "most powerful army in the world."

Also, Dorchester Heights remains free from the

TRENCH WARFARE, WHICH THE COLONISTS USED AT THE BATTLE OF BUNKER HILL, WAS RARE PRIOR TO THE AMERICAN REVOLUTIONARY WAR.

British invaders . . . for now.

I am uncertain now of my own fate as a soldier.

BUNKER HILL AND BREED'S HILL

To commemorate the Battle of Bunker Hill, citizens of the new United States erected a monument at the site. The monument is an obelisk and stands 221 feet (67.4 m). Visitors can climb an inside staircase to the top. It took 17 years to build and is made entirely of granite quarried from Quincy, Massachusetts. Marquis de Lafayette, a prominent Frenchman who helped the Continental Army win the war, returned to the United States on the 50th anniversary of the battle and laid the cornerstone of the monument in a special ceremony.

General George Washington has taken command of the Continental Army and has indicated that he will not allow African Americans to enlist.

I am told that a petition has been drafted citing my bravery and skill. It will be sent to the General Court of the Massachusetts Bay Colony. No other soldier at the Battle of Bunker Hill will receive such an honor, I am told.

The letter was signed by 14 officers, including General Prescott. It says that I "behaved like an experienced officer" and that in me "centers a brave and gallant soldier." I have been credited with fatally wounding two important British officers. To be cited for bravery and courage on the battlefield is no small thing. I am both humbled and proud to continue the fight, but I must await General Washington's final decision.

3

ABIGAIL ADAMS

BATTLE OF BUNKER HILL OBSERVER AND FUTURE UNITED STATES OF AMERICA FIRST LADY

I do not know how to write this letter, so great is my grief. Yet, I must inform my husband, John, who is away at Philadelphia meeting with the Continental Congress, of our great loss. One of our dearest friends, Dr. Joseph Warren, perished in the battle at Breed's Hill and Bunker Hill. I must admit, the violence of this battle shocks me. My young children are also heartbroken.

ABIGAIL ADAMS WAS BORN ABIGAIL SMITH ON NOVEMBER 22, 1744 IN WEYMOUTH, MASSACHUSETTS.

Ten-year-old Abigail, whom we call Nabby, and eight-year-old John Quincy are taking the loss very hard. Five-year-old Charles and two-year-old Thomas are too young to truly understand what happened. But I sense they feel my own grief. They are in quiet, grave moods.

At first, the children thought the sounds of battle were a mere thunderstorm. But the weather is warm and bright. There's not a storm cloud in sight. The

WOMEN IN THE COLONIES

Women played many roles during the colonists' battle for independence from Britain. Some of the roles were traditional, such as nurses, seamstresses, cooks, and maids. Other women took on more untraditional roles, including soldiers and spies. Deborah Sampson from Plympton, Massachusetts, dressed as a man and fought in New York under the alias Robert Shurtliff. Her identity was discovered in 1781. Hannah Blair, from North Carolina, helped protect and hide patriots and carried secret messages. She was given a pension for her work as a spy when the war was over.

"thunder" is the sound of artillery, cannonade from British warships anchored in the Charles River, and the pounding of musket shots and cannon fire on land. Now they are very afraid.

"Charlestown is laid in ashes," I write. The destruction is a great pity. The loss of so many lives, including our dear friend Dr. Warren, is nearly impossible to bear. I put pen to paper and try again. I consider telling John that Dr. Warren refused to take a commission for his part in the battle. Instead, he volunteered and insisted on fighting where the danger was greatest. But I am sure John already knows how very brave his lost friend was.

No one had greater ardor for the cause of liberty than Dr. Warren. When Dr. Warren wrote the Suffolk Resolves, he noted that "no obedience is due" to the Intolerable Acts. He encouraged us all to **boycott** and protest these oppressive measures. Also, few know this, but it was he who dispatched both Mr. Paul

JOSEPH WARREN DIED AT THE BATTLE OF BUNKER HILL AFTER HE WAS STRUCK IN THE HEAD BY A MUSKET BALL. HIS BODY WAS IDENTIFIED BY THE FALSE TOOTH MADE FOR HIM BY SILVERSMITH PAUL REVERE.

Revere and Mr. William Dawes on their midnight rides to warn the minutemen of imminent danger from the redcoats. Our dear Dr. Warren was also an extraordinary healer and a beloved family friend. He cared for my husband's cousin, Samuel Adams, our friend, John Hancock, and our own young, who were growing up as his patients. He also saw General Gage's wife and children as patients. Perhaps this allowed him access to information that the British would rather the colonial militia not know. But I will say no more of that here.

ANALYZE THIS

Analyze another account of the Battle of Bunker Hill in this book and compare it to this one. How are they alike? How are they different?

My words about Dr. Warren feel sad, empty. I do not truly have the power to convey the depth of our loss. But since I am a witness to this battle as it unfolds, perhaps I should share the details of fighting.

I write to John that the battle began with the

THE SON OF JOHN ADAMS, JOHN QUINCY ADAMS, THE SIXTH PRESIDENT OF THE UNITED STATES, WAS BORN IN THE ADAMS FAMILY HOME ON JULY 11, 1767. TODAY IT IS A MUSEUM RUN BY THE NATIONAL PARK SERVICE.

colonial militia taking over Breed's Hill and Bunker Hill under cover of darkness on June 16. The fighting began with the British attack on Bunker Hill at about 3 o'clock on June 17. It continues still, though it is now 3 o'clock in the afternoon on June 18.

For a long time, John Quincy and I watched the battle from atop a hill on our farm in nearby Braintree. John Quincy is especially affected by the violence that unfolds so close to our home. He held my hand and let his tears fall freely while we watched the battle together. How dearly I hope that this time of conflict is over before he is old enough to fight. This is unfair of me, I know, given the sons who lie dead on the battlefield. I cannot help how I feel. Perhaps if women had the right to an education and the right to vote, we would handle these delicate matters without violence. I will take it up with John. He must know as he works to form a new government that we ladies will not consider ourselves bound by any laws in

THINK ABOUT IT

Determine the main idea of this chapter and pick out one piece of evidence that supports it.

which we have no voice or representation. This is a sentiment all patriots must surely understand. But perhaps that is a letter for another time.

John Quincy and I were not the only ones to watch the violence play out. Our neighbors in Boston and surrounding towns and villages climbed church steeples, hills, and rooftops to watch the battle unfold. We are only 10 miles (16 kilometers) away from the fighting. If it comes closer, I will take the children and go to my brother-in-law's house for protection. But unless I really must move, I plan to stay here at the farm in Braintree, where there is much to be done in my husband's absence.

Who knew that I would ever be called upon to become a farmess? But with John gone for weeks, sometimes months at a time, I find myself taking on what would normally be his business affairs. I trade livestock and oversee planting and harvesting. I even buy land and hire help! With a great many women whose husbands serve as soldiers or politicians, I am

THE SALTBOX-STYLE HOUSE WHERE JOHN ADAMS WAS BORN ON OCTOBER 30, 1735 STILL STANDS NEXT DOOR TO JOHN QUINCY ADAMS'S BIRTHPLACE HOUSE.

not alone in undertaking these tasks that used to fall upon the shoulders of the men.

As I finish this letter, I must end on a positive note, so that John will know our spirits remain high. "The Spirits of the people are very good," I write. "The loss of Charlestown affects them no more than a drop in the bucket." Will John see through my false cheer? I hope not. We must all keep our chins up. I am much afraid that our situation will get worse before it gets better.

Word has reached me that the colonial militiamen at Breed's Hill and Bunker Hill fell into retreat because the men ran out of artillery. I must leave off now and set to work melting down my pewter dinnerware. It will make excellent musket balls.

A MAP THAT REVERSED THE TWO HILLS LED TO CONFUSION OVER THE NAME OF THE BATTLE. COLONEL PRESCOTT THOUGHT HE WAS ON BUNKER HILL DUE TO THE MISTAKE ON HIS MAP.

TIMELINE

BATTLE OF BUNKER HILL

The Quartering Act is passed. The law requires colonists to provide food and shelter, even in their own homes, for English soldiers living in the colonies.

MARCH 24, 1765

The Sons of Liberty, a secret group of patriots whose mission is to oppose unjust English laws, is formed. In Boston, the Sons of Liberty group is led by Samuel Adams.

JULY 1765

The Boston Massacre takes place. A crowd of jeering colonists taunts a British soldier. When other soldiers come to his aid, shots break out. Five colonists are killed.

MARCH 5, 1770

MARCH 1774

Parliament passes the Coercive Acts to punish the colonists for resisting British rule. These laws are meant to force colonists to bend to British rule. The colonists call these laws the Intolerable Acts.

APRIL 19, 1775

The Battles of Lexington and Concord take place.

JUNE 17, 1775

The British attack colonial militiamen on Breed's Hill and Bunker Hill. When the colonial militiamen run out of ammunition, the British win this battle. It is known as the Battle of Bunker Hill.

LOOK, LOOK AGAIN

Take a close look at this illustration of the Battle of Bunker Hill and answer the following questions:

1. What would a British general see in this picture? What would he think of American colonists waging a fight with the British Army? Would he see them as heroes or villains? Why?

2. How would the wife of a patriot describe this scene to her husband, who was away in Philadelphia working on creating a new government? What would the woman, who lived close to the fighting and had small children to care for, think when looking at this scene?

3. What would a former slave think about this scene? How would the free African American think differently from the soldier, who had never been a slave and had not had to buy his freedom?

GLOSSARY

artillery *(ahr-TILL-ur-ee)* weapons

barracks *(BAH-rakz)* a building or group of buildings used to house soldiers

boycott *(BOI-cot)* to refuse to buy, use, or participate in as a way of protesting

diplomatically *(dip-low-MAT-ick-lee)* related to the practice of negotiating with other nations

intolerable *(in-TOL-ur-able)* unbearable

Parliament *(PAR-le-ment)* an assemblage of the nobility, clergy, and commons called together by the British sovereign as the supreme legislative body in the United Kingdom

quartering *(KWOR-tur-ing)* being housed in a dwelling

Seven Years' War *(SEV-un YEERS WOR)* called the French and Indian War in the colonies, a war fought partly in America in which Austria, France, Sweden, and Russia fought Britain, Hanover, and Prussia for a number of territories

Sons of Liberty *(SUNZ UV lib-ur-TEE)* a secret group of patriots that protected and fought for the rights of colonists against the British government

treasonous *(TREE-zon-ous)* the offense of trying to overthrow a government to which a person owes allegiance

LEARN MORE

FURTHER READING

Burgan, Michael. *The Battle of Bunker Hill: An Interactive History Adventure.* Mankato, MN: Capstone Press, 2016.

Lüsted, Marcia Amidon. *The Battle of Bunker Hill: A History Perspectives Book.* Ann Arbor, MI: Cherry Lake Publishing, 2014.

Philbrick, Nathaniel. *Ben's Revolution: Benjamin Russell and the Battle of Bunker Hill.* New York: Nancy Paulsen Books, 2017.

WEBSITES

The Battle of Bunker Hill
https://www.history.com/topics/american-revolution/battle-of-bunker-hill
This website describes what happened during the Battle of Bunker Hill.

The Battle of Bunker Hill
https://www.britannica.com/event/Battle-of-Bunker-Hill
This website explains more about the Battle of Bunker Hill and offers information about other battles during the American Revolutionary War.

INDEX

ABOUT THE AUTHOR

Kristin J. Russo is a university English lecturer. She loves teaching, reading, writing, and learning new things. She and her husband live near Providence, Rhode Island, in a small house surrounded by flower gardens. They have three grown children and three rescue dogs.